Connected Mathematics™

Samples and Populations

Data and Statistics

Student Edition

Glenda Lappan
James T. Fey
William M. Fitzgerald
Susan N. Friel
Elizabeth Difanis Phillips

Developed at Michigan State University

DALE SEYMOUR PUBLICATIONS®
MENLO PARK, CALIFORNIA

Connected Mathematics™ was developed at Michigan State University with the support of National Science Foundation Grant No. MDR 9150217.

This project was supported, in part,
by the
National Science Foundation
Opinions expressed are those of the authors
and not necessarily those of the Foundation

The Michigan State University authors and administration have agreed that all MSU royalties arising from this publication will be devoted to purposes supported by the Department of Mathematics and the MSU Mathematics Education Enrichment Fund.

This book is published by Dale Seymour Publications®, an imprint of Addison Wesley Longman, Inc.
Dale Seymour Publications
2725 Sand Hill Road
Menlo Park, CA 94025
Customer Service (800) 872-1100

Managing Editor: Catherine Anderson
Project Editor: Stacey Miceli
Production/Manufacturing Director: Janet Yearian
Production/Manufacturing Coordinator: Claire Flaherty
Design Manager: John F. Kelly
Photo Editor: Roberta Spieckerman
Design: PCI, San Antonio, TX
Composition: London Road Design, Palo Alto, CA
Illustrations: Pauline Phung, Margaret Copeland, Ray Godfrey
Cover: Ray Godfrey

Photo Acknowledgements: 5 © Joseph Nettis/Photo Researchers, Inc.; 11 © Bob Daemmrich/Stock, Boston; 20 © Judy Gelles/Stock, Boston; 22 (both photos) Michael Dwyer/Stock, Boston; 24 © Tony Duffy/Allsport; 33 © Rick Lee/ Superstock; 45 © Doris DeWitt/Tony Stone Images; 49 © UPI/Corbis-Bettmann; 50 © Stuart Struever/Tony Stone Images; 56 © Reuters/Corbis-Bettmann; 65 © D. LaBelle/The Image Works

Order number 21485
ISBN 1-57232-190-3

3 4 5 6 7 8 9 10-BA-01 00 99

The Connected Mathematics Project Staff

Project Directors

James T. Fey
University of Maryland

William M. Fitzgerald
Michigan State University

Susan N. Friel
University of North Carolina at Chapel Hill

Glenda Lappan
Michigan State University

Elizabeth Difanis Phillips
Michigan State University

Project Manager

Kathy Burgis
Michigan State University

Technical Coordinator

Judith Martus Miller
Michigan State University

Curriculum Development Consultants

David Ben-Chaim
Weizmann Institute

Alex Friedlander
Weizmann Institute

Eleanor Geiger
University of Maryland

Jane Miller
University of Maryland

Jane Mitchell
University of North Carolina at Chapel Hill

Anthony D. Rickard
Alma College

Collaborating Teachers/Writers

Mary K. Bouck
Portland, Michigan

Jacqueline Stewart
Okemos, Michigan

Graduate Assistants

Scott J. Baldridge
Michigan State University

Angie S. Eshelman
Michigan State University

M. Faaiz Gierdien
Michigan State University

Jane M. Keiser
Indiana University

Angela S. Krebs
Michigan State University

James M. Larson
Michigan State University

Ronald Preston
Indiana University

Tat Ming Sze
Michigan State University

Sarah Theule-Lubienski
Michigan State University

Jeffrey J. Wanko
Michigan State University

Evaluation Team

Mark Hoover
Michigan State University

Diane V. Lambdin
Indiana University

Sandra K. Wilcox
Michigan State University

Judith S. Zawojewski
National-Louis University

Teacher/Assessment Team

Kathy Booth
Waverly, Michigan

Anita Clark
Marshall, Michigan

Julie Faulkner
Traverse City, Michigan

Theodore Gardella
Bloomfield Hills, Michigan

Yvonne Grant
Portland, Michigan

Linda R. Lobue
Vista, California

Suzanne McGrath
Chula Vista, California

Nancy McIntyre
Troy, Michigan

Mary Beth Schmitt
Traverse City, Michigan

Linda Walker
Tallahassee, Florida

Software Developer

Richard Burgis
East Lansing, Michigan

Development Center Directors

Nicholas Branca
San Diego State University

Dianne Briars
Pittsburgh Public Schools

Frances R. Curcio
New York University

Perry Lanier
Michigan State University

J. Michael Shaughnessy
Portland State University

Charles Vonder Embse
Central Michigan University

Special thanks to the students and teachers at these pilot schools!

Baker Demonstration School
Evanston, Illinois

Bertha Vos Elementary School
Traverse City, Michigan

Blair Elementary School
Traverse City, Michigan

Bloomfield Hills Middle School
Bloomfield Hills, Michigan

Brownell Elementary School
Flint, Michigan

Catlin Gabel School
Portland, Oregon

Cherry Knoll Elementary School
Traverse City, Michigan

Cobb Middle School
Tallahassee, Florida

Courtade Elementary School
Traverse City, Michigan

Duke School for Children
Durham, North Carolina

DeVeaux Junior High School
Toledo, Ohio

East Junior High School
Traverse City, Michigan

Eastern Elementary School
Traverse City, Michigan

Eastlake Elementary School
Chula Vista, California

Eastwood Elementary School
Sturgis, Michigan

Elizabeth City Middle School
Elizabeth City, North Carolina

Franklinton Elementary School
Franklinton, North Carolina

Frick International Studies Academy
Pittsburgh, Pennsylvania

Gundry Elementary School
Flint, Michigan

Hawkins Elementary School
Toledo, Ohio

Hilltop Middle School
Chula Vista, California

Holmes Middle School
Flint, Michigan

Interlochen Elementary School
Traverse City, Michigan

Los Altos Elementary School
San Diego, California

Louis Armstrong Middle School
East Elmhurst, New York

McTigue Junior High School
Toledo, Ohio

National City Middle School
National City, California

Norris Elementary School
Traverse City, Michigan

Northeast Middle School
Minneapolis, Minnesota

Oak Park Elementary School
Traverse City, Michigan

Old Mission Elementary School
Traverse City, Michigan

Old Orchard Elementary School
Toledo, Ohio

Portland Middle School
Portland, Michigan

Reizenstein Middle School
Pittsburgh, Pennsylvania

Sabin Elementary School
Traverse City, Michigan

Shepherd Middle School
Shepherd, Michigan

Sturgis Middle School
Sturgis, Michigan

Terrell Lane Middle School
Louisburg, North Carolina

Tierra del Sol Middle School
Lakeside, California

Traverse Heights Elementary School
Traverse City, Michigan

University Preparatory Academy
Seattle, Washington

Washington Middle School
Vista, California

Waverly East Intermediate School
Lansing, Michigan

Waverly Middle School
Lansing, Michigan

West Junior High School
Traverse City, Michigan

Willow Hill Elementary School
Traverse City, Michigan

Contents

Samples and Populations

The homecoming committee wants to estimate how many students will attend the homecoming dance, but they don't want to ask every student in the school. How could they select a sample of students to survey? How could they use the results of their survey to predict the number of students who will attend?

A cookie company claims that there are at least 1000 chips in every 1-pound bag of its chocolate chip cookies. How could you test this claim? How do you think the company guarantees this claim?

A radio talk-show host asked her listeners to call in to express their opinions about a local election. Do you think the results of this survey could be used to describe the opinions of all the show's listeners?

The U.S. census attempts to gather information from every household in the United States. Gathering, organizing, and analyzing data from such a large population is expensive and time-consuming. In most studies of large populations, data are gathered from a sample, or portion, of the population. The data from the sample are then used to make predictions or to draw conclusions about the population.

Sampling is an important tool in statistics and data analysis. Understanding how to select samples and how to use them to make predictions will help you when you consider questions like those on the opposite page.

Mathematical Highlights

In *Samples and Populations*, you will learn some new ways to summarize and display data, and you will learn how to use sampling to make predictions about large populations.

- By calculating five-number summaries and making box plots, you compare the distributions of quality ratings and prices for peanut butters with different attributes.

- Making a scatter plot allows you to explore the relationship between quality and price for several brands of peanut butter.

- As you devise plans for selecting samples of students, you learn about various sampling techniques and consider the advantages and disadvantages of each.

- Developing a survey to gather information about the future plans of students gives you practice at writing effective survey questions.

- Selecting random samples of students helps you estimate statistics about the sleep and movie-viewing habits of a large population of students and leads you to discover the relationship between sample size and the accuracy of statistical estimates.

- Using what you know about samples and populations, you solve a mystery involving arrowheads discovered at ancient Native American settlements.

- By generating random numbers, you simulate making chocolate chip cookies and help two bakers solve a quality-control problem.

Using a Calculator

In this unit, you may use a graphing calculator to make box plots and generate random numbers. As you work on the Connected Mathematics™ units, you decide whether to use a calculator to help you solve a problem.

Comparing Data Sets

American shoppers have a greater variety of stores and products to choose from than do shoppers anywhere else in the world. With so many choices, it can be difficult to decide which product to purchase. Many people turn to information in consumer surveys and product comparisons to help them make informed decisions.

A recent consumer survey rated 37 varieties of peanut butter. Each brand was assigned a quality rating from 1 to 100 points. A panel of trained tasters made two general statements about quality:

- Peanut butters with higher quality ratings were smooth; had a sweet, nutty flavor; and were not overly dry or sticky.
- Peanut butters with lower quality ratings were not very nutty; had small chunks of peanuts; or had a burnt or slightly rancid taste.

In addition to quality ratings, the article listed the sodium content and the price per 3-tablespoon serving for each brand. Brands were classified according to three attributes: natural or regular, creamy or chunky, and salted or unsalted. The data are presented in the table on the next page. A fourth attribute, name brand or store brand, has been added to the data.

Think about this!

- Who might be interested in the results of this peanut butter study?
- What interesting questions about peanut butter can be answered with these data?
- What interesting questions about peanut butter cannot be answered with these data?

Peanut Butter Comparisons

	Brand	Quality rating	Sodium per serving (mg)	Price per serving	Regular/ natural	Creamy/ chunky	Salted/ unsalted	Name brand/ store brand
1.	Smucker's Natural	71	15	27¢	natural	creamy	unsalted	name
2.	Deaf Smith Arrowhead Mills	69	0	32	natural	creamy	unsalted	name
3.	Adams 100% Natural	60	0	26	natural	creamy	unsalted	name
4.	Adams	60	168	26	natural	creamy	salted	name
5.	Laura Scudder's All Natural	57	165	26	natural	creamy	salted	name
6.	Country Pure Brand (Safeway)	52	225	21	natural	creamy	salted	store
7.	Hollywood Natural	34	15	32	natural	creamy	unsalted	name
8.	Smucker's Natural	89	15	27	natural	chunky	unsalted	name
9.	Adams 100% Natural	69	0	26	natural	chunky	unsalted	name
10.	Deaf Smith Arrowhead Mills	69	0	32	natural	chunky	unsalted	name
11.	Country Pure Brand (Safeway)	67	105	21	natural	chunky	salted	store
12.	Laura Scudder's All Natural	63	165	24	natural	chunky	salted	name
13.	Smucker's Natural	57	188	26	natural	chunky	salted	name
14.	Health Valley 100% Natural	40	3	34	natural	chunky	unsalted	name
15.	Jif	76	220	22	regular	creamy	salted	name
16.	Skippy	60	225	19	regular	creamy	salted	name
17.	Kroger	54	240	14	regular	creamy	salted	store
18.	NuMade (Safeway)	43	187	20	regular	creamy	salted	store
19.	Peter Pan	40	225	21	regular	creamy	salted	name
20.	Peter Pan	35	3	22	regular	creamy	unsalted	name
21.	A & P	34	225	12	regular	creamy	salted	store
22.	Food Club	33	225	17	regular	creamy	salted	store
23.	Pathmark	31	255	9	regular	creamy	salted	store
24.	Lady Lee (Lucky Stores)	23	225	16	regular	creamy	salted	store
25.	Albertsons	23	225	17	regular	creamy	salted	store
26.	Shur Fine (Shurfine Central)	11	225	16	regular	creamy	salted	store
27.	Jif	83	162	23	regular	chunky	salted	name
28.	Skippy	83	211	21	regular	chunky	salted	name
29.	Food Club	54	195	17	regular	chunky	salted	store
30.	Kroger	49	255	14	regular	chunky	salted	store
31.	A & P	46	225	11	regular	chunky	salted	store
32.	Peter Pan	45	180	22	regular	chunky	salted	name
33.	NuMade (Safeway)	40	208	21	regular	chunky	salted	store
34.	Lady Lee (Lucky Stores)	34	225	16	regular	chunky	salted	store
35.	Albertsons	31	225	17	regular	chunky	salted	store
36.	Pathmark	29	210	9	regular	chunky	salted	store
37.	Shur Fine (Shurfine Central)	26	195	16	regular	chunky	salted	store

Sources: "The Nuttiest Peanut Butter." *Consumer Reports* (September 1990): pp. 588–591.
A. J. Rossman, *Workshop Statistics: Student Activity Guide.* Carlisle, Penn.: Dickinson College, 1994, pp. 5–18.

1.1 Comparing Quality Ratings

To help determine which peanut butter is the
"best buy," you could make several comparisons.
For example, you could compare the quality
ratings of the regular brands with the quality
ratings of the natural brands, which contain
no preservatives. How would you summarize
and display the data to help you decide
whether natural brands or regular brands
have higher quality ratings?

Problem 1.1

Apply some of the data analysis techniques you learned in earlier statistics work
to compare the quality ratings for natural brands and regular brands.

In general, do natural brands or regular brands have higher quality ratings?
Use the results of your analysis to justify your choice.

■ Problem 1.1 Follow-Up

1. For the quality ratings of the regular brands, the mean is greater than the median.
Why do you think this is true?

2. For the quality ratings of the natural brands, the mean and the median are close
in value. Why do you think this is true?

1.2 Using Box-and-Whiskers Plots

Box-and-whiskers plots, or *box plots,* are useful representations of the distribution of
values in a data set. The box plot below shows the distribution of quality ratings for the
natural brands of peanut butter.

Quality Ratings for Natural Brands

Quality rating

A box plot is constructed from the five-number summary of the data. The **five-number summary** includes the minimum value, maximum value, median, lower quartile, and upper quartile.

You know how to find the minimum value, maximum value, and median in a set of data. The **lower quartile** is the median of the data values below the median. The **upper quartile** is the median of the data values above the median. The diagram below illustrates the five-number summary for the quality ratings of the natural brands of peanut butter.

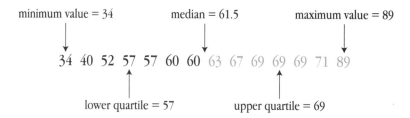

The plot below shows how the numbers in the five-number summary correspond to the features of the box plot.

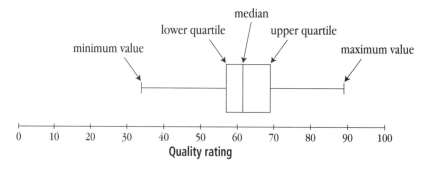

By displaying two or more box plots on the same scale, you can compare distributions. The box plots below allow you to compare the distributions of quality ratings for natural brands and regular brands.

Quality Ratings for Natural and Regular Brands

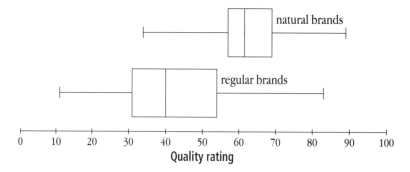

Problem 1.2

A. About what percent of the values in a data set are below the median? About what percent of the values in a data set are above the median?

B. The lower quartile, median, and upper quartile divide a data distribution into four parts. These four parts are called the *first*, *second*, *third*, and *fourth quartiles* of the distribution.

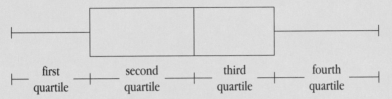

About what percent of the values in a data distribution are in each quartile?

C. Use the box plots of quality ratings for regular and natural brands to help you decide which type of peanut butter—regular or natural—is of higher quality. Explain your reasoning.

Problem 1.2 Follow-Up

Values in a data set that are much greater or much less than most of the other values are called *outliers*. To help you decide whether a value is an outlier, find the length of the box in a box plot of the data. The length of the box is the difference between the upper and lower quartiles. This length is called the *interquartile range*, abbreviated IQR. If a value is greater than 1.5 times the IQR added to the upper quartile or less than 1.5 times the IQR subtracted from the lower quartile, it is an outlier.

1. Are there outliers in the quality ratings for the natural brands? Are there outliers in the quality ratings for the regular brands?

2. On a box plot, outliers are sometimes indicated with asterisks (*). Both pairs of box plots below show the distribution of quality ratings for regular and natural brands of peanut butter. In the plots on the right, outliers have been indicated with asterisks.

Quality Ratings for Natural and Regular Brands

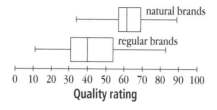

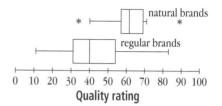

a. In the plots on the left, the whiskers extend from the box to the minimum and maximum values. What values do the whiskers in the plots on the right extend to?

b. Describe how you would construct a box plot if you wanted to show the outliers in a set of data.

1.3 Comparing Prices

Many people consider *both* quality and price when deciding which products or brands to buy. The box plots below show the distributions of per-serving prices for natural and regular brands of peanut butter.

Peanut Butter Prices

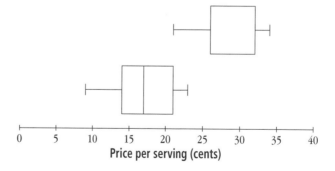

Problem 1.3

In the peanut butter data on page 6, refer to the column giving price per serving.

A. Calculate the five-number summary for the prices of the natural brands.

B. Calculate the five-number summary for the prices of the regular brands.

C. Compare the five-number summaries you found in parts A and B with the box plots shown on the previous page. Decide which plot shows the distribution of prices for the natural brands and which plot shows the distribution of prices for the regular brands. Explain how the numbers in the five-number summaries are shown by various features of the plots.

D. How do the prices of the natural brands compare with the prices of the regular brands? Explain how you can make this comparison by using the box plots.

E. If *price* were the only factor a buyer considered, would natural peanut butter or regular peanut butter be a better choice? If *quality* were the only factor a buyer considered, would natural peanut butter or regular peanut butter be a better choice? Explain your reasoning.

■ Problem 1.3 Follow-Up

1. About what percent of the data are in the box of a box plot? That is, what percent are between the upper and lower quartiles?

2. About what percent of the data are in the interval from the minimum value to the upper quartile?

3. About what percent of the data are in the interval from the lower quartile to the maximum value?

1.4 Making a Quality Choice

The 37 brands of peanut butter listed on page 6 are classified according to four attributes: natural or regular, creamy or chunky, salted or unsalted, and name brand or store brand. In Problems 1.1 and 1.2, you compared the quality ratings of regular brands with the quality ratings of natural brands. You found that natural brands are a good choice based on their quality ratings. In this problem, you will compare the quality ratings for the other three attributes.

Problem 1.4

Justify your answers to the questions below with statistics and box plots.

A. Compare the quality ratings of the creamy brands with the quality ratings of the chunky brands. Based on quality, are creamy brands or chunky brands a better choice?

B. Compare the quality ratings of the salted brands with the quality ratings of the unsalted brands. Based on quality, are salted brands or unsalted brands a better choice?

C. Compare the quality ratings of the name brands with the quality ratings of the store brands. Based on quality, are name brands or store brands a better choice?

▦ Problem 1.4 Follow-Up

1. List the four attributes—natural or regular, creamy or chunky, salted or unsalted, and name brand or store brand—you would recommend to someone who wants to choose a peanut butter based on quality ratings.

2. Can you find at least one brand of peanut butter in the list that has all the attributes you recommend?

1.5 Comparing Quality and Price

In previous problems, you explored the quality and price data for natural and regular peanut butters. You may have wondered how the price of a brand of peanut butter is related to its quality. What connection would you expect between price and quality for any product?

To explore the relationship between two variables, you can make a coordinate graph, or **scatter plot**. The scatter plot below shows the (quality rating, price) data for all 37 brands of peanut butter.

Peanut Butter Quality and Price

Problem 1.5

For these questions, refer to the quality ratings and per-serving prices in the table of peanut butter data on page 6.

A. In the graph above, which plot symbol, ● or ◆, represents data for natural peanut butter? Which represents data for regular peanut butter?

B. Is there an overall relationship between quality and price? Explain.

C. Do any (quality rating, price) data pairs appear to be unusual? Explain your reasoning.

D. In Problems 1.2 and 1.3, you used box plots to compare quality ratings and prices of natural and regular peanut butters.

1. How can you use the scatter plot to compare the quality ratings of the natural brands with the quality ratings of the regular brands?

2. How can you use the scatter plot to compare the prices of the natural brands with the prices of the regular brands?

■ Problem 1.5 Follow-Up

Some people are concerned about the
sodium content of the foods they eat.
People with heart and blood-pressure
problems are often put on low-sodium
diets. Notice in the table on page 6 how
the unsalted brands contain very little
sodium compared to the salted brands.
This is because table salt contains sodium.

1. Make a scatter plot of the (quality rating, sodium) data for all 37 brands of peanut butter. Use different symbols for salted brands and unsalted brands.

2. Does there appear to be an overall relationship between sodium content and quality rating? Explain.

3. Look back at the box plots you made of the quality ratings for the salted brands and of the quality ratings for the unsalted brands in part B of Problem 1.4. Is there a connection between quality rating and the salt content of peanut butter? Explain your thinking.

4. In questions 1–3, you looked for a relationship between quality rating and sodium content or added salt. Compare your conclusions about this relationship based on the scatter plot with your conclusions based on the box plots. What are the strengths and weaknesses of each type of data display?

As you work on these ACE questions, use your calculator whenever you need it.

Applications

1. Refer to the peanut butter data on page 6.

a. In Problem 1.3, you compared the prices of natural brands with the prices of regular brands. Based on price, are natural brands or regular brands a better choice?

b. Based on price, are creamy brands or chunky brands a better choice? Justify your answer with statistics and graphs.

c. Based on price, are salted brands or unsalted brands a better choice? Justify your answer with statistics and graphs.

d. Based on price, are name brands or store brands a better choice? Justify your answer with statistics and graphs.

e. List the four attributes—natural or regular, creamy or chunky, salted or unsalted, and name brand or store brand—you would recommend to someone who wants to choose a peanut butter based on price.

f. Can you find at least one brand of peanut butter that has all the attributes you recommend?

2. The scatter plot below shows (quality rating, sodium) data for the 37 brands of peanut butter listed on page 6.

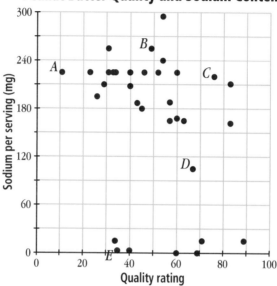

Peanut Butter Quality and Sodium Content

a. Compare the values in the table with the scatter plot. Why are some points located on or very near the horizontal axis?

b. Give the approximate coordinates of each labeled point. Explain what the coordinates tell you about the brand represented by the point.

3. The table on the next page gives the engine type, body length, and wingspan of several airplanes flown by major airlines.

a. Based on body length, how do propeller planes compare to jet planes? Justify your answers with statistics and graphs.

b. Based on wingspan, how do propeller planes compare with jet planes? Justify your answers with statistics and graphs.

4. Make a scatter plot of the (wingspan, body length) data given in the table on page 17. Describe the overall relationship between these two variables.

Airplane Data

Plane	Engine type	Body length (m)	Wingspan (m)
Boeing 707	jet	46.6	44.4
Boeing 747	jet	70.7	59.6
Ilyushin IL-86	jet	59.5	48.1
McDonnell Douglas DC-8	jet	57.1	45.2
Antonov An-124	jet	69.1	73.3
British Aerospace 146	jet	28.6	26.3
Lockheed C-5 Galaxy	jet	75.5	67.9
Antonov An-225	jet	84.0	88.4
Airbus A300	jet	54.1	44.9
Airbus A310	jet	46.0	43.9
Airbus A320	jet	37.5	33.9
Boeing 737	jet	33.4	28.9
Boeing 757	jet	47.3	38.1
Boeing 767	jet	48.5	47.6
Lockheed Tristar L-1011	jet	54.2	47.3
McDonnell Douglas DC-10	jet	55.5	50.4
Aero/Boeing Spacelines Guppy	propeller	43.8	47.6
Douglas DC-4 C-54 Skymaster	propeller	28.6	35.8
Douglas DC-6	propeller	32.2	35.8
Lockheed L-188 Electra	propeller	31.8	30.2
Vickers Viscount	propeller	26.1	28.6
Antonov An-12	propeller	33.1	38.0
de Havilland DHC Dash-7	propeller	24.5	28.4
Lockheed C-130 Hercules/L-100	propeller	34.4	40.4
British Aerospace 748/ATP	propeller	26.0	30.6
Convair 240	propeller	24.1	32.1
Curtiss C-46 Commando	propeller	23.3	32.9
Douglas DC-3	propeller	19.7	29.0
Grumman Gulfstream I/I-C	propeller	19.4	23.9
Ilyushin IL-14	propeller	22.3	31.7
Martin 4-0-4	propeller	22.8	28.4
Saab 340	propeller	19.7	21.4

Source: William Berk and Frank Berk. *Airport Airplanes.* Plymouth, Mich.: Plymouth Press, 1993.

Connections

5. The graphs below compare prices (in U.S. dollars) of 2-liter bottles of soft drink in cities around the world. The titles and the axis labels are missing.

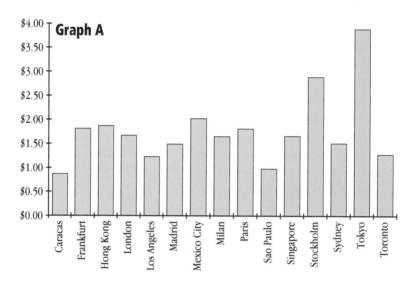

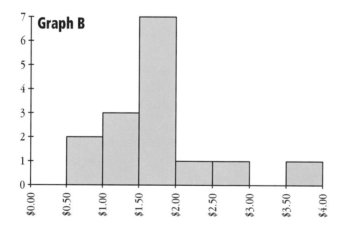

Source: Runzheimer International, Rochester, Wis., as reported in *Consumer Digest* (December, 1994): p. 8.

a. Which graph could you use to identify the cities with the highest and lowest soft-drink prices? Give the names of these cities and the prices.

b. Which graph could you use to find the typical price of a 2-liter bottle of soft drink for all the cities? What is the typical price? Explain how you found your answer.

c. What title and axis labels would be appropriate for each graph?

d. If you were given only graph A, would you have enough information to make graph B? Explain your reasoning.

e. If you were given only graph B, would you have enough information to make graph A? Explain your reasoning.

6. Two students were comparing snack-size boxes of two brands of raisins, TastiSnak and Nature's Best. The brands sell for the same price. Tim said that TastiSnak raisins are a better deal because there are more raisins in each box. Kadisha disagreed. She said that since a box of either brand contains half an ounce, the brands give you the same amount for your money.

To test these claims, the students determined the actual number of raisins and the mass in grams for 50 boxes of each brand. The results are shown in the box plots below. Based on the mass and the number of raisins, which brand is a better deal? Explain how you used the graphs to determine your answer.

Number of Raisins in Each Box

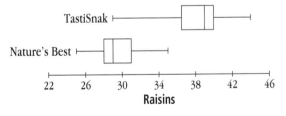

Mass of Raisins in Each Box

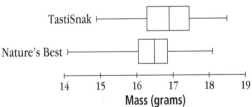

7. The sum of the values in a particular set of data is 250, and the mean is 25.

   a. Create a data set that fits this description.

   b. Do you think other students in your class created the same data set you did? Explain.

   c. Must the median of the data set be close in value to the mean? Explain.

Extensions

8. In many sports, the length of a game or match is determined by a time clock. In baseball, however, a game ends when nine innings have been completed and one team is ahead. If the teams are tied after nine innings, extra innings are played until one team is ahead. The graph below displays data about the duration of professional baseball games (in minutes). The title and the axis labels are missing.

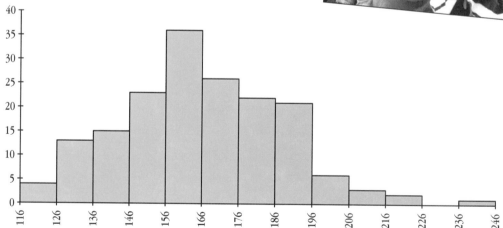

Source: *Student Poster Projects: Winners of the American Statistics Poster Competition, 1991–1992*. Palo Alto, Calif.: Dale Seymour Publications, 1994, p. 20.

a. What title and axis labels are appropriate for this graph?

b. What does the shape of the graph tell you about the length of a typical baseball game?

c. About how many games are represented in the graph?

d. Estimate the lower quartile, the median, and the upper quartile for these data. What do these numbers tell you about the length of a typical baseball game?

9. The scatter plot below shows (body length, wingspan) data for jet and propeller planes. The plot shows that, in general, greater body lengths are associated with greater wingspans. It's often useful to model such a trend with a linear graph and an equation.

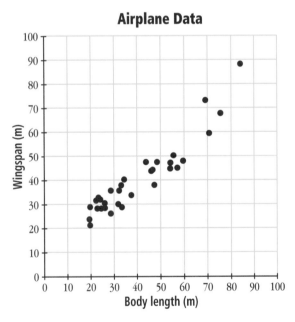

a. The line that passes through (0, 0) and (100, 100) is a good model for this data. Draw this line on the (body length, wingspan) scatter plot on Labsheet 1.ACE.

b. Write an equation for the line.

c. What are the slope and the y-intercept of the line? What does the slope tell you about the relationship between body length and wingspan?

d. What can you conclude about the wingspan and body length of an airplane that is represented by a point *above* the line?

e. What can you conclude about the wingspan and body length of an airplane that is represented by a point *below* the line?

f. What can you conclude about the wingspan and body length of an airplane that is represented by a point *on* the line?

Mathematical Reflections

In this investigation, you reviewed your knowledge of statistics and data displays. You learned how to use the five-number summary of a data set to make a box plot. And, you used box plots to compare data distributions. These questions will help you summarize what you have learned:

1 Describe how you would construct a box plot for a set of data.

2 **a.** What is true about the values in a data set if the mean is *greater than* the median?

  b. What is true about the values in a data set if the mean is *close in value* to the median?

  c. What is true about the values in a data set if the mean is *less than* the median?

3 How can you use box plots to compare two or more data sets?

4 **a.** In what types of situations is a scatter plot useful?

  b. Describe how you would construct a scatter plot.

Think about your answers to these questions, discuss your ideas with other students and your teacher, and then write a summary of your findings in your journal.

Conducting Surveys

If you wanted to gather information about students in your class—such as their preferences for food, television programs, music, or sports—it would be fairly easy to conduct an accurate survey. But what might you do if you wanted information about all the students in your school, or all the people in your city, your state, or the entire country?

Some recent reports made these claims:

- Americans spend 44% of their food budget on meals prepared away from home.
- Of all restaurant orders, 49% are for off-premises consumption.
- More than 2 million American youths, most of them girls, participate in competitive gymnastics.
- On Tuesday, July 30, 1996, more than 45 million American households watched evening broadcasts of the Atlanta Olympic Games.

Think about this!

How could the people who reported these data know about the eating, sports, and television-viewing activities of all 260 million Americans?

You can study a large **population** by collecting data from a small part, or **sample,** of that population. You can then *make predictions* or *draw conclusions* about the entire population based on data from the sample. The challenge in such studies is to find a sample that accurately represents the population. Such a sample is called a **representative sample**.

2.1 Asking About Honesty

Newspapers, magazines, and radio and television programs conduct surveys on a variety of subjects. Such surveys often ask readers or listeners to call in to express their views. A magazine with a national circulation asked its readers to phone in their answer to five questions about honesty.

How Honest Is America?

A. If you found someone else's wallet on the street, would you
  1. try to return it to the owner?
  2. return it, but keep the money?
  3. keep the wallet and the money?

B. If a cashier mistakenly gave you $10 extra in change, would you
  1. tell the cashier about the error?
  2. say nothing and keep the cash?

C. Would you cheat on an exam if you were sure you wouldn't get caught?
  1. yes
  2. no

D. If you found someone else's telephone calling card, would you use it?
  1. yes
  2. no

E. Do you feel that you are an honest person in most situations?
  1. yes
  2. no

Call 1-900-555-8281, and enter your answers by pressing the appropriate number keys.

Problem 2.1

A. A *sampling plan* is a strategy for choosing a sample from a population. What is the sampling plan for this survey? What are the population and the sample for this survey?

B. Suppose 5280 people answered the survey, and 4224 of them pressed 2 for question C. What percent of the callers said they would not cheat on an exam?

C. Of the 5280 callers, 1584 pressed 1 for question D. What percent of the callers said they would not use someone else's calling card?

D. The U.S. population is about 260 million. Based on the results of this survey, how many people in the United States would not cheat on an exam? How many would not use someone else's calling card?

E. List some reasons why predictions about all Americans based on this survey might be inaccurate.

■ **Problem 2.1 Follow-Up**

1. The magazine conducting the survey assumes a person is honest if he or she reports honest behavior for all five questions. Suppose that, according to these criteria, 3507 people out of the 5280 who responded are honest. Based on these results, what percent of the U.S. population would you predict is honest?

2. Write two questions that could be used to gather additional information about honest behavior.

3. How could you revise the sampling plan for this survey so you would be more confident that the results would predict the percent of the U.S population that is honest?

2.2 Selecting a Sample

The results of the telephone survey in Problem 2.1 were used to make predictions about the U.S. population. Making accurate predictions about a population based on the results of a survey can be complicated, even when you are interested in a relatively small population.

Suppose you are doing a research project on the lives of students at your school and would like to answer these questions:

- How many hours of sleep do students get each night?
- How many students eat breakfast in the morning?
- How many hours of television do students watch in a week?
- How many soft drinks do students consume in a day?
- How many students wear braces on their teeth?

If your school has a large student population, it might be difficult to gather and analyze information from every student. How could you select a sample of your school population to survey?

Problem 2.2

Ms. Baker's class wants to find out how many students in their school wear braces on their teeth. The class divides into four groups. Each group devises a plan for sampling the school population.

- Each member of group 1 will survey the students who ride on his or her school bus.

- Group 2 will survey every fourth person in the cafeteria line.

- Group 3 will read a notice on the school's morning announcements asking for volunteers for their survey.

- Group 4 will randomly select 30 students for their survey from a list of three-digit student ID numbers. They will roll a 10-sided number cube three times to generate each number.

A. What are the advantages and disadvantages of each sampling plan?

B. Which plan do you think would most accurately predict the number of students in the school who wear braces? That is, which plan do you think will give the most *representative* sample? Explain your answer.

■ Problem 2.2 Follow-Up

The plans developed by the groups in Ms. Baker's class are examples of common sampling methods.

1. Group 1's plan is an example of **convenience sampling.** What do you think convenience sampling is? Describe another plan that would use convenience sampling.

2. Group 2's plan is an example of **systematic sampling.** What do you think systematic sampling is? Describe another plan that would use systematic sampling.

3. Group 3's plan is an example of **voluntary-response sampling.** What do you think voluntary-response sampling is? Describe another plan that would use voluntary-response sampling.

4. Group 4's plan is an example of **random sampling.** What do you think random sampling is? Describe another plan that would use random sampling.

5. When using sampling methods to study a large population, it is important to choose samples that are representative of the population. Samples that give misleading impressions are called **biased samples.** Which groups in Problem 2.2 are likely to get a biased sample? Explain your answers.

6. Which sampling method was used in Problem 2.1?

2.3 Asking the Right Questions

You have seen that when conducting a survey, it is important to select a representative sample. You must also be careful about how you ask your questions.

When you write a survey, you need to think about whether each question should be an open question or a closed question.

An *open question* asks a person to write a response. Here are two examples of open questions:

> What is your age?
>
> After high school, what do you plan to do?

The first question has predictable responses that should be easy to organize and analyze. Although answers to the second question are less predictable, the question gives the person the freedom to answer in any way he or she chooses.

A *closed question* provides a person with a set of choices. Here, the two questions above are restated as closed questions:

What is your age?

_____ under 12	_____ 12	_____ 13	_____ 14
_____ 15	_____ 16	_____ 17	_____ over 17

After high school, which of the following do you plan to do?

_____ attend a two-year college	_____ join the service
_____ attend a four-year college	_____ get a full-time job
_____ attend a trade or vocational school	_____ other

The answers to closed questions are generally easier to organize and analyze than the answers to open questions, but closed questions limit the possible responses.

When you critique a survey you have written, you should ask yourself several things:

- Are the questions clearly stated?
- Can any of the questions be misinterpreted?
- Have I provided good, reasonable choices for the closed questions in my survey?
- What types of answers can I expect to the open questions?
- Will I be able to organize and analyze the data I collect?

Problem 2.3

In this problem, you will work with a partner to design a survey to gather information about middle school and high school students and their plans for the future. Your survey should include questions about characteristics of the students, such as age, gender, and favorite school subject. Your survey should also gather information about what students plan to do after graduation from high school. For example, your survey might include questions about the following topics:

• Students' plans for college or a job immediately after high school

• The types of careers students would like to pursue

• The places students would like to live

A. Work with a partner to develop a first draft of a survey. Exchange surveys with another pair of students, and critique each other's survey.

B. Prepare a final version of your survey.

C. Write a paragraph describing a sampling plan you could use to survey students in your school.

■ Problem 2.3 Follow-Up

1. At Hilltop Middle School, there are 200 sixth graders, 200 seventh graders, and 200 eighth graders. If you gave your survey to one class of 25 students in each grade, could you use the results to make predictions about all the students in the school? Explain your reasoning.

2. At Valleyview Middle School, there are 250 sixth graders, 250 seventh graders, and 250 eighth graders. About 60% of the students at each grade level are girls. How could you select a random sample of students in the school so that 60% of the students in your sample are girls and 40% are boys?

As you work on these ACE questions, use your calculator whenever you need it.

Applications

There are 350 students in Banneker Middle School. Mr. Abosch's math class wants to find out how many hours of homework a typical student in the school did last week. Several students in the class devised plans for selecting a sample of students to survey. In 1–4, tell whether you think the plan would give a representative sample, and explain your answer.

1. Anna suggested surveying every third student on each homeroom class list.

2. Kwang-Hee suggested putting 320 white beans and 30 red beans in a bag and asking each student to draw a bean as he or she enters the auditorium for tomorrow's assembly. The 30 students who draw red beans will be surveyed.

3. Ushio suggested that each student in Mr. Abosch's class survey everyone in his or her English class.

4. Kirby suggested putting surveys on a table at the entrance to the school and asking students to return completed questionnaires at the end of the day.

In 5–8, describe the population being studied and the sampling method being used.

5. A magazine for teenagers asks its readers to write in with information about how they solve personal problems.

6. To find out how much time middle school students spend on the telephone each day, members of an eighth grade class kept a record for a week of the amount of time they spent on the phone each day.

7. To estimate the number of soft drinks consumed by middle school students each day, Ms. Darnell's class obtains a list of students in the school and writes each name on a card. They put the cards in a box and select the names of 40 students to survey.

8. A television news report said that 80% of adults in the United States support the right of school authorities to open student lockers to search for drugs, alcohol, and weapons. The editors of the school paper want to find out how students in their school feel about this issue. They select 26 students for their survey—one whose name begins with A, one whose name begins with B, one whose name begins with C, and so on.

9. Choose one of the issues in questions 5–8. Write a survey question you could ask about the issue, and explain how you could analyze and report the results you collect.

Connections

10. Students at Banneker Middle School were asked how much time they spent doing homework last Monday night. The results are shown in this back-to-back stem-and-leaf plot.

Minutes Spent on Monday-Night Homework

Grade 6		Grade 8
0 0 0 0 0 0	0	0
5 5 5 5 5 5	1	0 5 5
5 0 0	2	0 0 0 5 5 5
5 5 5	3	0 0 0 0 5 5 5
5 5 0	4	0 0 0 5 5 5
0 0	5	0 5
	6	0 5 5
0	7	5
5	8	0

a. Find the median homework time for each grade.

b. For each grade, describe the overall distribution of homework times. How do the homework times for sixth graders compare with the homework times for eighth graders? Explain your reasoning.

c. Could these data be used to describe what is typical of all school nights in each of the two grades? Explain your reasoning.

11. Samples of adults and eighth grade students were asked how much time they spend on the telephone each evening. The results are displayed in the box plots below.

Telephone Time

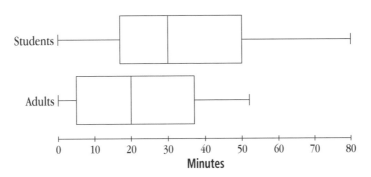

a. What are the median, lower quartile, upper quartile, and range of the telephone times for the students?

b. What are the median, lower quartile, upper quartile, and range of the telephone times for the adults?

c. Describe the similarities and differences between the distribution of telephone times for adults and the distribution of telephone times for students.

12. There are 350 students in Banneker Middle School. Ms. Cabral's class wants to research how many students attended camp last summer. They survey two random samples of students. Here are the results:

Sample 1: 8 of 25 attended camp

Sample 2: 7 of 28 attended camp

a. Based on the results from sample 1, how many students in the school would you predict attended camp?

b. Based on the results from sample 2, how many students in the school would you predict attended camp?

c. Lawrence, one of Ms. Cabral's students, was confused by the results of the study. He said, "We were careful to choose our samples randomly. Why did the two samples give us different predictions?" How would you answer Lawrence's question?

13. A local television station wanted to find out how the people in the broadcast area felt about women serving in combat roles in the military. During its evening news broadcast, the station asked viewers to call in with their opinions about this question:

Should women be allowed to have combat roles in the military?

a. What possible biases could there be in the results of this opinion poll?

b. Why do you think the media conduct such polls, even though they know the results are biased?

Extensions

14. Television stations, radio stations, and newspapers often predict the winners of important elections long before the votes are counted. They make these predictions based on polls.

    a. What factors might cause a preelection poll to be inaccurate?

    b. Political parties often conduct their own preelection polls to find out what voters think about their campaign and their candidates. How might a political party bias such a poll?

    c. Find out how a local television station, radio station, or newspaper takes preelection polls. Do you think the method they use is sensible?

15. In times of war, our government has set up a selective-service, or draft, system to identify young men who will be called into military service. For reasons of fairness, the selective-service system must make every effort to be sure that everyone eligible for the draft has the same chance of being selected. What do you think would be a fair system for selecting people to be drafted?

Mathematical Reflections

In this investigation, you learned about several sampling techniques, and you practiced writing effective survey questions. These questions will help you summarize what you have learned:

1 Why are data often collected from a sample rather than from an entire population?

2 Describe several methods for selecting a sample from a population. Discuss the advantages and disadvantages of each method.

3 a. What does it mean for a sample to be *representative* of a population?

b. In what ways might a sample *not* be representative of a population?

Think about your answers to these questions, discuss your ideas with other students and your teacher, and then write a summary of your findings in your journal.

INVESTIGATION 3

Random Samples

What is the best way to choose a sample from a large population? In most situations, statisticians agree that it is preferable to use a procedure that gives each member of the population the same chance of being chosen. Sampling plans with this property are called *random sampling plans*. Samples chosen with a random sampling plan are called *random samples*.

3.1 Choosing Randomly

This problem will help you think about what it means to use a random sampling plan. Keep in mind that for a sampling plan to be random, all members of the population must have an equally likely chance of being selected.

Problem 3.1

Imagine that you have two tickets to a sold-out rock concert, and your six best friends all want to go with you. To choose a friend to attend the concert, you want to use a strategy that gives each friend an equally likely chance of being selected. Which of the three strategies below would accomplish this? Explain your reasoning.

Strategy 1: The first person who calls you on the phone tonight gets to go with you.

Max Productions presents: **RAWLY & THE ZOOSTERS** WORLD JAMMIN' TOUR Saturday November 23 AT THE ORANGEVILLE COLISEUM	SECTION B 27 AA ROW SEAT RAWLY & THE ZOOSTERS WORLD JAMMIN' TOUR 8:00pm Saturday November 23 THE ORANGEVILLE COLISEUM

Strategy 2: You assign each friend a different whole number from 1 to 6. Then, you roll a six-sided number cube. The number that is rolled determines who attends the concert.

Strategy 3: You tell each friend to meet you by the rear door right after school. You toss a coin to choose between the first two friends who arrive.

■ **Problem 3.1 Follow-Up**

Describe another strategy you could use that would give each of your friends an equally likely chance of being selected.

3.2 Selecting a Random Sample

The table on the next page contains data for 100 eighth graders at Clinton Middle School. The data were collected on a Monday. They include the number of hours of sleep each student got the previous night and the number of movies, including television movies and videos, each student watched the previous week.

You could describe these data by calculating five-number summaries or means, and you could display the distribution of the data by making stem plots, histograms, or box plots. However, doing calculations and making graphs for the entire data set would require a lot of work.

Think about this!

Instead of working with the entire data set, you can select a random sample of students. You can look for patterns in the data for the sample and then use your findings to make predictions about the population.

- What methods might you use to select a random sample of students?

- How many students would you need in your sample in order to make accurate estimates of the typical number of hours of sleep and the typical number of movies watched for the entire population of 100 students?

One way to select a random sample of students is to use two spinners like these:

 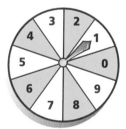

You can use the spinners to generate random pairs of digits that correspond to the two-digit student numbers. What two-digit numbers can you generate with these spinners? How can you make sure that student 100 has an equally likely chance of being included in your sample?

There are many other ways to select a random sample of students. For example, you can roll two 10-sided number cubes, or you can generate random numbers with your calculator.

Grade 8 Database

Student number	Gender	Sleep (hours)	Movies	Student number	Gender	Sleep (hours)	Movies
01	boy	11.5	14	51	boy	5.0	4
02	boy	2.0	8	52	boy	6.5	5
03	girl	7.7	3	53	girl	8.5	2
04	boy	9.3	1	54	boy	9.1	15
05	boy	7.1	16	55	girl	7.5	2
06	boy	7.5	1	56	girl	8.5	1
07	boy	8.0	4	57	girl	8.0	2
08	girl	7.8	1	58	girl	7.0	7
09	girl	8.0	13	59	girl	8.4	10
10	girl	8.0	15	60	girl	9.5	1
11	boy	9.0	1	61	girl	7.3	5
12	boy	9.2	10	62	girl	7.3	4
13	boy	8.5	5	63	boy	8.5	3
14	girl	6.0	15	64	boy	9.0	3
15	boy	6.5	10	65	boy	9.0	4
16	boy	8.3	2	66	girl	7.3	5
17	girl	7.4	2	67	girl	5.7	0
18	boy	11.2	3	68	girl	5.5	0
19	girl	7.3	1	69	boy	10.5	7
20	boy	8.0	0	70	girl	7.5	1
21	girl	7.8	1	71	boy	7.8	0
22	girl	7.8	1	72	girl	7.3	1
23	boy	9.2	2	73	boy	9.3	2
24	girl	7.5	0	74	boy	9.0	1
25	boy	8.8	1	75	boy	8.7	1
26	girl	8.5	0	76	boy	8.5	3
27	girl	9.0	0	77	girl	9.0	1
28	girl	8.5	0	78	boy	8.0	1
29	boy	8.2	2	79	boy	8.0	4
30	girl	7.8	2	80	boy	6.5	0
31	girl	8.0	2	81	boy	8.0	0
32	girl	7.3	8	82	girl	9.0	8
33	boy	6.0	5	83	girl	8.0	0
34	girl	7.5	5	84	boy	7.0	0
35	boy	6.5	5	85	boy	9.0	6
36	boy	9.3	1	86	boy	7.3	0
37	girl	8.2	3	87	girl	9.0	3
38	boy	7.3	3	88	girl	7.5	5
39	girl	7.4	6	89	boy	8.0	0
40	girl	8.5	7	90	girl	7.5	6
41	boy	5.5	17	91	boy	8.0	4
42	boy	6.5	3	92	boy	9.0	4
43	boy	7.0	5	93	boy	7.0	0
44	girl	8.5	2	94	boy	8.0	3
45	girl	9.3	4	95	boy	8.3	3
46	girl	8.0	15	96	boy	8.3	14
47	boy	8.5	10	97	girl	7.8	5
48	girl	6.2	11	98	girl	8.5	1
49	girl	11.8	10	99	girl	8.3	3
50	girl	9.0	4	100	boy	7.5	2

Problem 3.2

In this problem, each member of your group will select a random sample of students and calculate the five-number summary for the movie data. Use spinners, 10-sided number cubes, a graphing calculator, or some other method to select your sample.

A. Select a random sample of 25 students. For each student in your sample, record the number of movies watched. (Each sample should contain 25 *different* students, so if you select a student who is already in the sample, select another.)

B. Calculate the five-number summary for the movie data for your sample.

C. With your group, make box plots of the movie data for your group's samples on Labsheet 3.2.

D. What can you conclude about the movie-viewing behavior of the population of 100 students based on the patterns in the samples selected by your group? Explain how you used the data from your samples to arrive at your conclusions.

E. Compare your findings with those of other groups in your class. Describe the similarities and differences you find.

■ Problem 3.2 Follow-Up

1. Select a random sample of 25 students, and record the number of hours of sleep for each student. Calculate the five-number summary for these sleep data, and make a box plot of the distribution. Use your findings to estimate the typical hours of sleep for the population of 100 students. Compare your box plot and estimate with those of the other members of your group, and describe the similarities and differences.

2. The data on page 39 were collected by conducting a survey. The students who wrote the survey considered two possible questions for finding the number of movies watched.

- How many movies and videos did you watch last week?
- How many movies did you watch at a theater, on television, or on video last week? Include all movies and videos you watched from last Monday through this Sunday.

a. Which question do you think is better? Why?

b. Can you write a better question? If so, write one, and explain why you think your question is better.

3.3 Choosing a Sample Size

In Problem 3.2, you selected random samples of 25 students to estimate the sleep and movie-viewing habits of all 100 students. You might wonder whether you could make good estimates with less work by selecting smaller samples.

If you took the time to analyze the movie data for all 100 students, you would find that the median number of movies and videos watched is 3. Do you think you could make a good estimate of this figure by analyzing samples of 5 or 10 students?

Problem 3.3

In this problem, you will explore how the size of a sample affects the accuracy of statistical estimates.

A. In Problem 3.2, you calculated five-number summaries for the movie data for random samples of 25 students. Work with your class to make a line plot of the medians found by all groups. Compare these results with the median for the population of 100 students.

B. 1. Select three random samples of 5 students, and find the median movie value for each sample. Compare the medians for your samples with the population median.

    2. Compare the medians for your samples with the medians found by other members of your group. Describe the similarities or differences you find.

    3. Record the medians found by your group on the board. When all groups have recorded their medians, make a line plot of the medians.

C. 1. Select three random samples of 10 students, and find the median movie value for each sample. Compare the medians for your samples with the population median.

    2. Compare the medians for your samples with the medians found by other members of your group. Describe the similarities or differences you find.

    3. Record the medians found by your group on the board. When all groups have recorded their medians, make a line plot of the medians.

D. Compare the distribution of medians for samples of size 5, 10, and 25. Write a paragraph describing how the median estimates for samples of different sizes compare with the actual population median.

■ Problem 3.3 Follow-Up

1. With your class, use the sleep data to explore the relationship between sample size and the accuracy of median estimates. The median sleep value for the population of 100 students is 8 hours.

a. In Problem 3.2 Follow-Up, you calculated the median sleep value for random samples of 25 students. Work with your class to make a line plot of the medians found by all the students in your class. Compare these results with the median for the population.

b. Select a random sample of 5 students and a random sample of 10 students. Find the median sleep value for each sample.

c. Work with your class to make a line plot of the medians for the samples of 5 students and a line plot for the samples of 10 students.

d. Compare the distribution of medians for samples of size 5, 10, and 25. How do the median estimates for samples of different sizes compare with the median for the population?

2. If each student in your class chose a sample of 50 students and found the median sleep value, what would you expect the line plot of the medians to look like? Explain your reasoning.

As you work on these ACE questions, use your calculator whenever you need it.

Applications

1. **a.** Refer to the data on page 39. Select three random samples from the population of 100 students: one sample of 5 students, one sample of 10 students, and one sample of 25 students. Record the sleep values for the students in each sample.

b. Calculate the mean sleep value for each sample.

c. Your teacher will display axes for three line plots: one for means for samples of size 5, one for means for samples of size 10, and one for means for samples of size 25. Add your data to the line plots.

d. The mean sleep value for the population is 7.96 hours. Compare this value with the estimates shown in the three line plots. Write a paragraph describing how the mean estimates for samples of different sizes compare with the mean for the population.

2. **a.** Refer to the data on page 39. Select three random samples from the population of 100 students: one sample of 5 students, one sample of 10 students, and one sample of 25 students. Record the movie values for the students in each sample.

b. Calculate the mean movie value for each sample.

c. Your teacher will display axes for three line plots: one for means for samples of size 5, one for means for samples of size 10, and one for means for samples of size 25. Add your data to the line plots.

d. The mean movie value for the population is 4.22. Compare this value with the estimates shown in the three line plots. Write a paragraph describing how the mean estimates for samples of different sizes compare with the mean for the population.

In 3–6, use this information: Manufacturers often conduct quality-control tests to ensure that their products perform well and are safe. Depending on the type of item and the quantity produced, a manufacturer may test every item or select samples to test. For each situation described below, imagine that you are the quality-control manager for the company. Describe the testing program that you would recommend, and justify your recommendation.

3. Happy Bug Toys produces 5000 video-game systems each day.

4. The Spartan Music company manufactures a total of about 200,000 compact discs for 100 recording artists each day.

5. Fourth of July Fireworks, Incorporated, produces rockets used in fireworks displays. In the spring and early summer, they produce more than 1500 rockets each day.

6. The Clear Spring bottling company produces 25,000 bottles of spring water each day.

Connections

7. Consider the following data set: 20, 22, 23, 23, 24, 24, 25.

a. Find the mean and the range of the values.

b. Add three values to the data set so that the mean of the new data set is greater than the mean of the original data set. What is the range of the new data set?

c. Add three values to the original data set so that the mean of the new data set is less than the mean of the original data set. What is the range of the new data set?

d. Look at the ranges for the original data set and the data sets you created in parts b and c. How do the ranges compare? Why do you think this is so?

8. A geyser is a spring from which columns of boiling water and steam erupt. The data displayed in the graph below were collected for the Grand Geyser in Yellowstone National Park. Each point represents the height of an eruption and the time since the previous eruption.

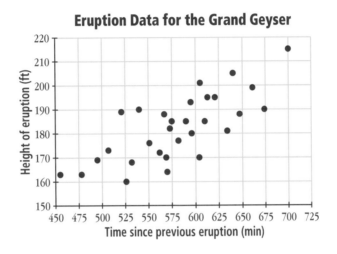

Eruption Data for the Grand Geyser

Height of eruption (ft) vs. *Time since previous eruption (min)*

a. Describe the overall relationship between the height of an eruption and the time since the previous eruption.

b. The data above were collected for one particular geyser. What additional information would you need to decide whether the relationship you described in part a is true for most geysers?

9. a. Suppose that instead of choosing random samples of 25 students from the population of 100 students, you selected the first 25 students for the first sample, the next 25 students for the second sample, and so on. How might this sampling procedure bias the statistical results?

b. Suppose you had chosen your samples systematically, by choosing students 1, 5, 9, 13, 17, 21, 25, . . . for the first sample; students 2, 6, 10, 14, 18, 22, 26, . . . for the second sample; students 3, 7, 11, 15, 19, 23, 27, . . . for the third sample; and so on. How might this sampling procedure bias the statistical results?

Extensions

10. Polls conducted prior to presidential elections commonly use samples of about 1000 eligible voters.

a. There are about 190 million eligible voters in the United States. What percent of eligible voters are in a sample of 1000?

b. How do you think this small sample is chosen so that the results will predict the winner with reasonable accuracy?

11. M&M's® candies are coated in six colors: green, yellow, orange, blue, brown, and red. The company produces a fixed percent of each color, but the percents are not equal. The table on the next page shows the distribution of colors in 100 bags of plain M&M's candies.

a. From the table, select random samples of 5, 15, and 25 bags, and use the samples to estimate the percent of red candies in a typical bag of M&M's.

b. Calculate the percent of red M&M's in all 100 bags. Which sample from part a produced a percent estimate closest to the overall percent? Why do you think that sample gave the closest estimate?

Data from 100 Bags of Plain M&M's Candies

Bag	Green	Yellow	Orange	Blue	Brown	Red	Total	Bag	Green	Yellow	Orange	Blue	Brown	Red	Total
1	3	10	9	5	10	18	55	51	9	9	6	6	17	10	57
2	5	12	4	6	19	11	57	52	4	13	4	6	17	13	57
3	7	10	9	4	16	12	58	53	6	12	3	8	13	12	54
4	4	14	2	1	14	19	56	54	11	8	8	12	9	8	56
5	12	7	8	7	14	13	61	55	1	16	7	3	22	10	59
6	10	9	6	5	15	8	55	56	6	11	6	4	19	11	57
7	11	11	6	6	12	12	58	57	7	7	7	3	10	21	55
8	8	15	5	3	16	10	57	58	7	2	8	10	15	13	55
9	2	11	4	4	24	12	57	59	6	10	6	7	12	15	56
10	5	7	4	1	26	13	56	60	6	16	7	3	16	9	57
11	6	13	4	4	15	18	60	61	6	10	4	5	23	10	58
12	5	8	4	2	23	16	58	62	10	7	2	6	19	9	53
13	9	13	4	4	14	11	55	63	4	12	8	6	10	15	55
14	9	10	5	5	14	14	57	64	9	12	8	6	8	15	58
15	5	19	5	2	13	14	58	65	10	6	5	4	12	16	53
16	3	15	5	2	19	11	55	66	4	11	3	2	21	15	56
17	3	10	4	3	23	14	57	67	6	15	4	8	10	10	53
18	6	7	5	5	15	22	60	68	6	8	7	1	19	14	55
19	5	7	3	4	21	14	54	69	6	8	8	6	10	16	54
20	8	7	8	2	20	16	61	70	9	11	7	4	15	10	56
21	10	11	7	7	8	14	57	71	6	9	8	2	19	14	58
22	7	10	3	5	20	12	57	72	3	10	9	5	10	18	55
23	3	8	6	3	25	10	55	73	5	12	4	6	19	11	57
24	6	11	9	3	10	17	56	74	7	10	9	4	16	12	58
25	10	12	1	2	15	17	57	75	4	14	2	1	16	19	56
26	4	12	4	7	14	16	57	76	1	8	10	1	22	14	56
27	6	9	6	7	15	13	56	77	5	15	4	9	11	11	57
28	5	11	6	7	17	7	53	78	3	11	6	3	24	10	57
29	1	10	6	5	22	14	58	79	10	9	4	1	23	10	57
30	10	4	8	0	26	9	57	80	5	10	7	1	21	13	57
31	4	14	6	4	18	12	58	81	6	14	7	7	14	5	53
32	6	18	2	4	19	14	58	82	9	11	2	6	13	16	57
33	6	7	8	4	20	11	56	83	7	7	9	0	13	20	56
34	12	11	6	4	11	11	55	84	8	10	4	5	13	10	50
35	5	10	6	2	12	16	51	85	4	11	2	1	24	15	57
36	8	9	4	4	16	17	58	86	4	12	6	3	21	12	58
37	2	12	2	6	11	21	54	87	5	8	7	4	20	13	57
38	5	7	3	4	21	19	59	88	7	11	7	7	13	10	55
39	8	7	8	2	20	16	61	89	9	11	4	2	12	18	56
40	10	11	7	7	8	14	57	90	4	15	8	4	16	10	57
41	7	10	3	5	20	12	57	91	7	11	6	4	18	11	58
42	3	8	6	3	23	10	50	92	5	8	8	3	20	12	56
43	6	11	9	3	10	17	56	93	7	3	2	6	26	11	55
44	10	12	1	2	15	17	57	94	9	6	3	1	28	12	59
45	5	13	2	4	22	11	57	95	12	11	9	2	18	5	58
46	6	10	9	5	14	13	57	96	9	11	3	3	17	12	55
47	6	16	7	3	16	9	57	97	5	12	6	5	17	13	58
48	6	10	4	5	23	10	58	98	4	11	9	3	21	10	58
49	10	7	2	6	19	9	53	99	11	12	5	3	17	9	57
50	4	12	8	6	10	15	55	100	6	16	6	6	16	4	54

Mathematical Reflections

In this investigation, you made predictions about a population by examining data for random samples. These questions will help you summarize what you have learned:

1 How are random samples different from convenience, voluntary-response, and systematic samples?

2 Why is random sampling preferable to convenience, voluntary-response, and systematic sampling?

3 Describe three methods for selecting a random sample from a given population. What are the advantages and disadvantages of each method?

4 If several random samples are selected from the same population, what similarities and differences would you expect to find in the medians, means, ranges, and quartiles of the samples?

5 How does the size of a sample affect its accuracy in estimating statistics for a large population?

Think about your answers to these questions, discuss your ideas with other students and your teacher, and then write a summary of your findings in your journal.

Solving Real-World Problems

In this investigation, you will apply what you have learned about statistics to two real-world problems.

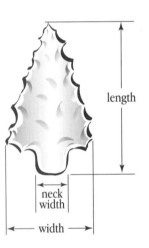

length

neck
width

width

4.1 Solving an Archaeological Mystery

Archaeologists study past civilizations by excavating ancient settlements and examining the artifacts of the people who lived there. On digs in southeastern Montana and north-central Wyoming, archaeologists discovered the remains of two Native American settlements. They unearthed a number of arrowheads at both sites. The tables on the next page list the length, width, and neck width for each arrowhead that was found. All measurements are in millimeters.*

*Source: George C. Knight and James D. Keyser. "A Mathematical Technique for Dating Projectile Points Common to the Northwestern Plains." *Plains Anthropologist 28*, no. 101 (1983): pp. 199–207.

Arrowheads from Two New Sites

Site I: 15 arrowheads		
Length	Width	Neck width
62	26	14
31	32	16
40	25	16
63	29	18
37	23	11
24	19	8
29	22	12
38	22	12
29	19	11
45	22	11
27	19	10
31	16	12
38	26	14
45	28	15
55	22	13

Site II: 37 arrowheads					
Length	Width	Neck width	Length	Width	Neck width
16	13	7	15	11	7
13	10	6	25	13	7
22	14	10	43	14	9
19	12	8	22	13	8
24	11	8	24	13	8
20	12	7	21	11	7
26	15	11	28	11	6
19	13	9	16	12	8
25	15	10	24	14	10
17	15	9	25	24	7
22	13	9	28	13	9
22	13	9	20	12	9
27	14	8	18	12	10
23	14	9	32	12	8
26	14	10	24	13	8
24	15	9	23	15	9
25	13	7	24	12	7
26	14	11	24	15	8
42	16	11			

The archaeologists hoped to use the arrowhead data to estimate the time period during which each site was inhabited. To help them, they used arrowhead data from four other settlement sites. The archaeologists knew that two of the sites—Laddie Creek/Dead Indian Creek and Kobold/Buffalo Creek—were settled between 4000 B.C. and A.D. 500, and that the other two sites—

Big Goose Creek and Wortham Shelter—were settled between A.D. 500 and A.D. 1600. The arrowhead data for these four sites are given on the next page.

Think about this!

How could you use these data to help you guess the settlement periods for the new sites?

Arrowheads from Four Old Sites

Big Goose Creek 52 Arrowheads		
Length	Width	Neck width
30	14	8
21	11	7
24	14	9
18	13	8
30	15	11
27	13	9
39	18	12
33	13	7
22	13	10
26	11	8
23	13	8
20	11	6
21	12	7
26	14	9
16	13	9
30	14	8
23	14	9
34	15	9
27	13	9
22	13	8
30	11	7
22	12	9
27	14	9
18	12	7
33	15	9
28	15	9
25	13	7
24	14	11
31	12	8
30	14	9
35	14	10
25	14	8
26	12	12
30	13	8
19	11	8
40	14	8
29	15	8
20	12	8
17	13	8
25	13	8
16	14	10
17	13	10
23	13	9
18	15	11
27	17	13
28	13	7
28	10	5
26	16	10
21	12	9
18	12	8
18	13	7
27	14	9

Wortham Shelter 45 Arrowheads		
Length	Width	Neck width
22	14	8
42	18	7
28	14	10
31	13	10
25	15	12
20	13	8
20	14	10
25	15	10
19	12	9
28	13	11
29	13	10
29	14	9
18	11	8
27	15	11
32	15	10
24	13	10
31	14	11
26	13	10
19	14	10
30	14	11
25	14	10
31	16	12
31	14	10
24	12	9
28	16	12
35	18	14
22	12	9
23	14	11
23	15	11
27	14	10
30	16	9
31	17	12
19	14	10
26	15	12
23	13	11
27	14	8
25	14	8
19	16	14
29	14	9
26	13	9
25	15	10
29	17	12
20	15	11
32	14	7
30	17	11

Laddie Creek/Dead Indian Creek: 18 Arrowheads		
Length	Width	Neck width
29	20	13
25	18	13
32	16	10
52	21	16
29	14	11
35	20	15
27	20	14
37	17	13
44	18	13
38	17	14
27	20	13
39	18	15
41	15	11
30	23	13
40	18	11
32	19	10
31	18	11
42	22	12

Kubold/Buffalo Creek 52 Arrowheads		
Length	Width	Neck width
80	25	11
38	24	15
39	21	14
50	23	15
42	22	14
37	21	11
32	23	18
44	20	11
40	20	12
40	20	13
56	19	12
52	17	12
46	23	14
32	22	17
35	22	14
46	20	14
38	18	9
40	21	12
46	17	13
44	20	12
40	19	15
30	19	15
31	17	12
31	16	13
32	20	13
41	21	13
25	18	15
49	20	14
35	19	11
42	22	15
44	25	14
47	19	13
47	22	13
45	22	13
54	24	13
56	21	15
37	18	12
51	18	10
71	24	13
45	20	13
52	24	16
67	21	13
47	20	12
50	23	16
56	25	13
50	21	13
52	22	15
57	22	15
61	19	12
66	20	15
64	21	13
30	17	12

Problem 4.1

The archaeologists hypothesized that Native Americans inhabiting the same area of the country during the same time period would have fashioned similar tools.

A. Use what you know about statistics and data representations to compare the lengths of the arrowheads discovered at the new sites with the lengths of the arrowheads from the known sites. Based on your comparisons, during which time period—4000 B.C. to A.D. 500 or A.D. 500 to A.D. 1600—do you think site I was settled? During which time period do you think site II was settled? Explain how your statistics and graphs support your answers.

B. Compare the widths of the arrowheads discovered at the new sites with the widths of the arrowheads from the known sites. Do your findings support your answers from part A? Explain.

C. If the archaeologists had collected only a few arrowheads from each new site, might they have reached a different conclusion? Explain your answer.

■ Problem 4.1 Follow-Up

1. Select a random sample of 15 arrowheads from each of the six sites. For each arrowhead, find the ratio of length to width. Express each ratio as a decimal rounded to the hundredths place.

2. Compare the length-to-width ratios for the various sites. Do the ratios help you match the new sites with the sites whose settlement time is known? Explain your answer.

4.2 Simulating Cookies

Jeff and Ted operate the Custom Cookie Counter in Durham Mall. Their advertising slogan is "Five giant chips in every cookie!" One day, a customer complained that she found only three chips in her cookie. Jeff said the customer must have miscounted because he mixes 60 chips into every batch of a dozen cookies. Jeff and Ted examined a batch of cookies that were fresh from the oven. The drawing on the right shows what they found.

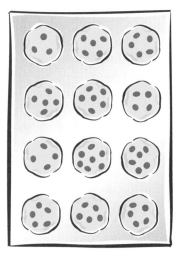

What is wrong with Jeff's reasoning about how many chips to add to each batch of cookie dough? What advice would you give to Jeff and Ted to help them solve their quality-control problem?

Ted had an idea about how to use random sampling to determine how many chips they should add to each batch of dough in order to be fairly confident that every cookie will contain at least five chips. He explained his idea to Jeff:

"Think about a batch of dough as 12 cookies packed in a bowl. As chips are added to the dough, each chip lands in one of the cookies. There is an equally likely chance that a chip will land in any one of the 12 cookies. We need to add chips to the dough until every cookie contains at least five chips."

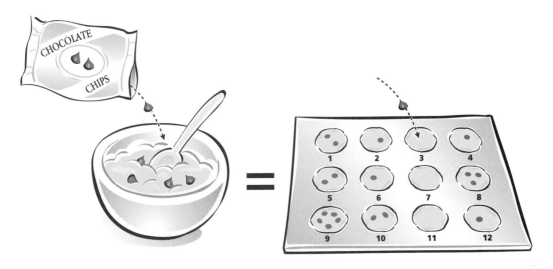

"We can simulate adding the chips by generating random integers from 1 to 12. Generating a 1 is equivalent to adding a chip to cookie 1, generating a 2 is equivalent to adding a chip to cookie 2, and so on. We can keep a tally of where the chips land and stop when each 'cookie' contains at least five 'chips.' The total number of random integers we generated will be an estimate of the number of chips we need to add to each batch to be fairly confident that each cookie will contain at least five chips."

Problem 4.2

Study Ted's plan for simulating the cookie mixing until it makes sense to you.

A. Conduct the simulation Ted describes. You might use a chart like this to tally the number of chips in each cookie.

cookie 1 _____
cookie 2 _____
cookie 3 _____
cookie 4 _____
cookie 5 _____
cookie 6 _____
cookie 7 _____
cookie 8 _____
cookie 9 _____
cookie 10 _____
cookie 11 _____
cookie 12 _____

Generate random numbers until each cookie contains at least five chips. When you are finished, find the total number of chips in the entire batch.

B. Your teacher will display the stem values for a stem plot. Add your number-of-chips data to the plot.

C. Jeff and Ted want to be quite certain there will be at least five chips in each cookie, but they don't want to waste money by mixing in too many chocolate chips. Based on your class data, how many chips would you advise Jeff and Ted to use in each batch? Explain how you determined your answer.

■ Problem 4.2 Follow-Up

1. What other methods might Jeff and Ted use to be fairly confident that each cookie they sell contains at least five chips?

2. As Jeff and Ted's business becomes more successful, they decide it would be more efficient to make cookies in batches of four dozen. How many chips should they add to each batch to be confident that each cookie has at least five chips?

3. How many chips would Jeff and Ted have to put in a batch of 12 cookies to be *absolutely certain* no cookie will have fewer than five chips?

As you work on these ACE questions, use your calculator whenever you need it.

Applications

1. The arrowhead data on pages 50 and 51 include the neck width of each arrowhead found in the six archaeological sites.

neck width

a. Calculate five-number summaries of the neck width for each site's arrowhead data. Based on these statistics, what conclusions can you draw about the time periods in which the new sites were settled?

b. On the same scale, make box plots of the neck-width data for all the sites. Explain how the relationships among the plots illustrate your conclusions from part a.

2. Oatmeal-raisin cookies are the most popular cookie at Jeff and Ted's Custom Cookie Counter. Jeff and Ted bake these cookies in batches of four dozen. They pour a box of raisins into each batch.

a. How could you use a sample of the cookies to estimate the number of raisins in a box?

b. If there are 1000 raisins in a box, how many raisins would you expect to find in a typical cookie?

3. Keisha opened a bag containing 60 chocolate chip cookies. She selected a sample of 20 cookies and counted the chips in each cookie.

Cookie	Chips
1	6
2	8
3	8
4	11
5	7
6	6
7	6
8	7
9	11
10	7

Cookie	Chips
11	8
12	7
13	9
14	9
15	8
16	6
17	8
18	10
19	10
20	8

Use the data from Keisha's sample to estimate the number of chips in the bag. Explain your answer.

4. The tables on page 57 list age and height data for the 1995 rosters of two professional basketball teams, the Houston Rockets and the Chicago Bulls.

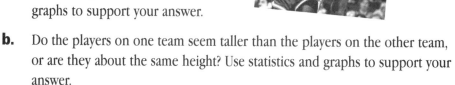

a. Do the players on one team seem older than the players on the other team, or are they about the same age? Use statistics and graphs to support your answer.

b. Do the players on one team seem taller than the players on the other team, or are they about the same height? Use statistics and graphs to support your answer.

c. Based on the data for these two teams, what estimates could you make for the age and height distributions of a typical NBA team? What cautions would you suggest in making generalizations from the given data?

Houston Rockets				Chicago Bulls		
Player	Age	Height (cm)		Player	Age	Height (cm)
Breaux	25	198		Armstrong	28	185
Brown	27	200		Blount	26	205
Cassell	26	188		Buechler	27	195
Chilcutt	27	208		Harper	31	195
Drexler	33	198		Jordan	33	198
Elie	32	193		Kerr	30	188
Herrera	29	203		Krystakowiak	31	203
Horry	25	205		Kukoc	27	208
Jones	38	203		Longley	26	215
Maxwell	30	190		Myers	32	195
Murray	24	198		Perdue	30	210
Olajuwon	32	210		Pippen	30	198
Smith	30	188		Simpkins	23	205
Tabak	25	210		Wennington	32	210

Connections

5. The U.S. Department of Transportation provides money to help states build new highways. However, there are strings attached. For example, if states fail to enforce the speed limits on interstate highways, they could lose their federal funding. To monitor driving speeds, states set up radar checkpoints to measure the speeds of samples of drivers.

a. Suppose you wanted to show that drivers in your state generally obey speed limits. Where and when would you set up radar checkpoints?

b. Suppose you wanted to show that drivers in your state often exceed speed limits. Where and when would you set up radar checkpoints?

6. Graphs are often used to support statistical arguments. However, sometimes graphs can be misleading. The graphs below all display the same data about the increase in newspaper recycling.

    a. Which graph do you think gives the most honest picture of the data pattern? Why?

    b. Why are the other graphs misleading?

Percent of Newspapers Recycled, 1980–1991

Graph W

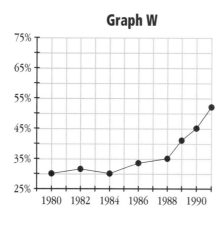

Graph X

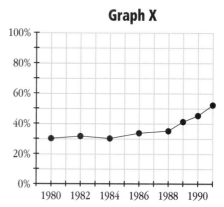

Graph Y

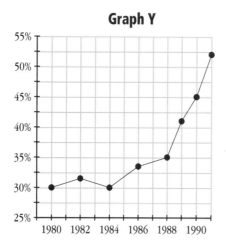

Graph Z

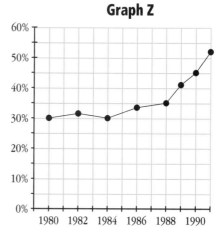

Even if you never have a job that requires you to design or analyze surveys, you will hear and read about surveys that interest you or that affect your daily life. When you are dealing with a survey, it is a good idea to ask yourself these questions:

- What was the goal of this survey?
- What was the population being studied?
- How was the sample chosen?
- How have the data been analyzed and reported?
- Do the data seem to support the conclusions?

In 7–11, use these and other relevant questions to analyze the survey.

7. In designing a television remote-control device, representatives for a manufacturer called 1000 households with television sets. They found that remote-control users sit an average of 3 meters from their television sets. Based on these findings, the manufacturer designed the remote control to work well at distances of 2.5 meters to 3.5 meters from a television set.

8. A lightbulb manufacturer wanted to know the "defect rate" for its product. One morning, the quality-control manager took 10 boxes of 50 lightbulbs from the assembly line and tried them in test sockets. All but 5 bulbs worked, so the manager concluded that production quality was acceptable.

9. A nutritionist wanted to estimate what percent of the calories in a typical U.S. teenager's diet were from fat. She asked health teachers in Dallas, Texas, to have their students keep logs of what they ate on one school day. The nutritionist analyzed the students' logs and found that the median intake was 500 fat calories per day, which is the recommended daily allowance. She concluded that calories from fat are not a problem in the diets of teenagers.

10. The Nabisco Company claims that there are over 1000 chocolate chips in a one-pound bag of ChipsAhoy!® cookies. A skeptical consumer asked how the company knew this was true. A spokesperson said that the company chose a sample of bags of cookies, soaked each bag in cold water to remove all the cookie dough, and weighed the chips that remained. In each case, the chips weighed more than a bag of 1000 chocolate chips.

11. In the cafeteria line, a student wrinkled his nose when he saw that salami-and-cheese subs were being served for lunch. When the cook asked what he would prefer, he replied, "I like bologna better." The cook asked the next ten students in line if they preferred bologna to salami. Seven students said yes, so she decided that in the future she would serve bologna subs instead of salami subs.

Extensions

12. Plain M&M's® candies are produced in the following percents.

Color	Percent in plain M&M's
brown	30%
yellow	20%
red	20%
orange	10%
green	10%
blue	10%

Suppose you are setting a table for a holiday party. You are placing small cups of M&M's candies at each place setting. Each cup contains 50 candies poured from a large bag of plain M&M's candies.

a. How many candies of each color would you expect to be in a typical cup?

b. How would you expect the number of candies of each color to vary across the samples?

c. You can simulate filling the cups with M&M's candies by generating random integers from 1 to 10. Which numbers would you let represent each color? How many random numbers would you need to generate to simulate filling one cup?

d. Carry out the simulation described in part c three times. Compare the distributions of colors in your simulated samples with the expected distribution from part a.

e. If you selected a random sample of 1000 candies from a large bag of plain M&M's candies, how closely would you expect the percent of each color in your sample to match the percents given in the table?

13. If you select five students at random from your class, what is the probability that at least two will have the same birth month? You can use a simulation to help you answer this question.

NOVEMBER						
SUN	**MON**	**TUE**	**WED**	**THU**	**FRI**	**SAT**
					1	2
3	4	5	6	7	8	9
10	11	12	13	14	15	16
17	18	19	20	21	22	23
24	25	26	27	28	29	30

a. Design a simulation to model this situation. Tell which month each simulation outcome represents.

b. Use your birth-month simulation to produce at least 25 samples of five people. Use your results to estimate the probability that at least two people in a group of five will have the same birth month.

c. Explain how you could revise your simulation to explore this question: What are the chances that at least two students in a class of 25 have the same birthday?

Mathematical Reflections

In this investigation, you applied your knowledge of statistics and data displays to two real-world problems. These questions will help you summarize what you have learned:

1 How can you use descriptive statistics such as the median, mean, range, and quartiles to compare samples and to draw conclusions about the populations from which they were selected?

2 In what ways can you expect the distribution of data values for a sample to be similar to and different from the distribution of data values for the entire population?

3 What rule of thumb can you use in thinking about the role of sample size in making accurate estimates of population properties?

Think about your answers to these questions, discuss your ideas with other students and your teacher, and then write a summary of your findings in your journal.

The Unit Project

Part 1: Safe Water and Life Expectancy

In most areas in the United States, tap water is safe to drink and purified drinking water is sold in grocery stores. In many countries, however, people do not have access to safe drinking water. In this project, you will explore the relationship between life expectancy and access to safe water.

Use the data in the table below and your knowledge of statistics and data representations to prepare a report that summarizes the relationship between life expectancy and access to safe drinking water.

Country	Region	Life expectancy (years)	Percent of people with access to safe water
Oman	Near East/South Asia	49	52
Yemen, Arab Republic	Near East/South Asia	43	4
Yemen	Near East/South Asia	46	37
Afghanistan	Near East/South Asia	37	10
Bangladesh	Near East/South Asia	48	68
Kampuchea	Near East/South Asia	39	45
Laos	Far East/Pacific	43	48
Nepal	Near East/South Asia	45	11
Angola	Africa	42	17
Central African Republic	Africa	43	18
Chad	Africa	43	26
Congo	Africa	43	26
Ethiopia	Africa	46	13
Guinea	Africa	43	10
Ivory Coast	Africa	47	14
Madagascar	Africa	48	26
Malawi	Africa	44	44
Mali	Africa	45	23
Mauritania	Africa	44	17
Mozambique	Africa	49	7

Country	Region	Life expectancy (years)	Percent of people with access to safe water
Niger	Africa	45	49
Nigeria	Africa	49	28
Rwanda	Africa	46	38
Senegal	Africa	44	35
Sierra Leone	Africa	47	9
Somalia	Africa	39	38
Sudan	Africa	47	46
Togo	Africa	48	11
Uganda	Africa	48	16
Upper Volta	Africa	44	14
Canada	Western Hemisphere	75	99
United States	Western Hemisphere	75	99
Argentina	Western Hemisphere	71	60
Costa Rica	Western Hemisphere	73	81
Cuba	Western Hemisphere	73	62
Jamaica	Western Hemisphere	71	82
Panama	Western Hemisphere	71	83
Trinidad and Tobago	Western Hemisphere	72	89
Uruguay	Western Hemisphere	71	78
Belgium	Western Europe	73	89
Denmark	Western Europe	75	99
France	Western Europe	76	97
Western Germany	Western Europe	73	99
Greece	Near East/South Asia	74	97
Italy	Western Europe	74	86
The Netherlands	Western Europe	76	97
Norway	Western Europe	76	98
Portugal	Western Europe	72	92
United Kingdom	Western Europe	74	99
Czechoslovakia	Eastern Europe	72	78
East Germany	Eastern Europe	73	82
Hungary	Eastern Europe	71	44
Poland	Eastern Europe	73	55
Austria	Eastern Europe	73	88
Finland	Western Europe	75	84
Ireland	Western Europe	73	73
Spain	Western Europe	74	78
Sweden	Western Europe	77	99
Switzerland	Western Europe	76	96
Yugoslavia	Western Europe	71	58
Israel	Near East/South Asia	73	99
Japan	Far East/Pacific	77	98
Singapore	Far East/Pacific	72	100
Australia	Far East/Pacific	74	97
New Zealand	Far East/Pacific	74	93

Source: David Nelson, Geroge Gheverghese Joseph, and Julian Williams. *Multicultural Mathematics.*
New York: Oxford University Press, 1993, pp. 178 and 179.

Part 2: Estimating Populations

The three drawings below represent fields of Canadian geese. Each dot represents one goose. A 10-by-10 grid has been placed over each drawing. Use what you know about random samples and data analysis to estimate the total number of geese in each field without counting all the geese. Prepare a report describing your methods and your findings.

Field A

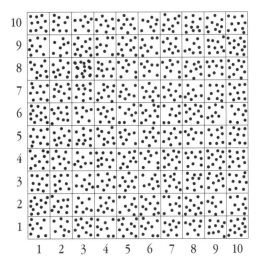

Field B

Field C

Glossary

biased sample A sample that does not accurately represent the population. Biased samples can give misleading results. If you wanted to predict how many students in your school recycle their soda cans, surveying only the ecology club would give you a biased sample.

box-and-whiskers plot (or box plot) A display that shows the distribution of values in a data set. A box plot is constructed from the five-number summary of the data. The box plot below shows the distribution of quality ratings for natural brands of peanut butter.

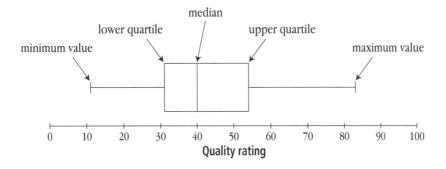

convenience sample A sample that is selected because it is convenient. If you survey everyone on your soccer team who attends tonight's practice, you are surveying a convenience sample.

distribution The arrangement of values in a data set.

five-number summary The minimum value, lower quartile, median, upper quartile, and maximum value for a data set. These five values give a summary of the shape of a distribution. The five-number summary for the quality ratings for regular brands of peanut butter is as follows:

  minimum value = 11
  lower quartile = 31
  median = 40
  upper quartile = 54
  maximum value = 83

histogram A display that shows the distribution of continuous data. The range of data values, divided into intervals, is displayed on the horizontal axis. The height of the bar over each interval indicates the number of data values in that interval. The histogram below shows quality ratings for regular brands of peanut butter. The height of the bar over the interval from 20 to 30 is 4. This indicates that four brands of peanut butter have quality ratings between 20 and 30.

Quality of Regular Brands

population The entire collection of people or objects you are studying.

random sample A sample chosen in a way that gives every member of a population an equally likely chance of being selected.

representative sample A sample that accurately represents a population.

sample A group of people or objects selected from a population. You can study a large population by collecting data from a sample. You can make predictions or draw conclusions about the entire population based on data from the sample.

scatter plot A graph used to explore the relationship between two variables. The graph below is a scatter plot of (length, wingspan) data for several airplanes. Each point represents the length and wingspan for one airplane.

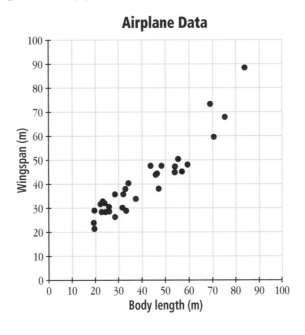

stem-and-leaf plot (or stem plot) A display that shows the distribution of values in a data set. Unlike a box plot or a histogram, a stem plot allows you to see the individual values in the data set. The stem plot below shows the distribution of quality ratings for regular brands of peanut butter. In this plot, the *stems* are a vertical list of the tens digits of the ratings. Attached to each stem are the corresponding *leaves,* in this case the ones digits. The leaves 3, 3, 6, and 9 next to the stem 2 indicate that the data set includes the values 23, 23, 26, and 29.

Quality Ratings of Regular Brands

```
0 |
1 | 1
2 | 3 3 6 9
3 | 1 1 3 4 4 5
4 | 0 0 3 5 6 9
5 | 4 4
6 | 0
7 | 6
8 | 3 3
9 |
```

Key
2 | 6 means 26.

systematic sample A sample selected in a methodical way. If you survey every tenth person on an alphabetical list of names, you are surveying a systematic sample.

voluntary-response sample A sample that selects itself. If you put an ad in the school paper asking for volunteers to take a survey, the students who respond will be a voluntary-response sample.

Index